Dear mummy + Ellen,

for mothers day 1998

22/3/98

Love Christopher and Jom

VEGETARIAN
GRILLING

VEGETARIAN GRILLING

HAMLYN

First published in 1997
by Hamlyn
an imprint of Reed Consumer Books Limited
Michelin House, 81 Fulham Road, London SW3 6RB
and Auckland, Melbourne, Singapore and Toronto

Copyright © 1997 Reed International Books Limited

ISBN 0 600 59277 4

Printed in China

CONVERSION CHART

OVEN TEMPERATURES RECOMMENDED EQUIVALENTS			CONVERSIONS FROM CUPS TO IMPERIAL AND METRIC			
°C	°F	Gas Mark	**Solid Measures**		Terminology	
110	225	¼	**American**	**Imperial and Metric**	**American**	**English**
120	250	½	2 cups butter or	1 lb/500 g	All-purpose Flour	Plain Flour
140	275	1	margarine		Confectioners' Sugar	Icing Sugar
150	300	2	4 cups flour	1 lb/500 g	Cornstarch	Cornflour
160	325	3	2 cups granulated or	1 lb/500 g	Corn Syrup	Golden Syrup
180	350	4	caster sugar		Golden Raisins	Sultanas
190	375	5	3 cups icing sugar	1 lb/500 g	Molasses	Black Treacle
200	400	6	1 cup rice	8 oz/250 g	Self-rising Flour	Self-raising Flour
220	425	7			Superfine Sugar	Caster Sugar
230	450	8	**Liquid Measures**		Sweet Butter	Unsalted Butter
240	475	9			Turbinado Sugar	Demerara Sugar
			American	**Imperial and Metric**		
			⅔ cup	¼ pint/150 ml		
			1¼ cups	½ pint/300 ml		
			2 cups	¾ pint/450 ml		
			2½ cups	1 pint/600 ml		
			3¾ cups	1½ pints/900 ml		
			5 cups	2 pints/1200 ml		

Notes
1 Use whole milk unless otherwise stated. 2 Use sweet (unsalted) butter unless otherwise stated.
3 Use medium-size vegetables unless otherwise stated.

Contents

Grilled Vegetables

Grilling is healthy and fun, especially outdoors on a barbecue. Cooking vegetables over charcoal or hardwood gives them a delicious smoky flavor. The delicate taste of eggplants and zucchini is enhanced by the slightly blackened skins when grilled over hot coals; the natural sweetness of colorful bell peppers is revealed; and the robust flavors of root vegetables, onions and garlic are stronger and more pungent.

Whether you cook over hot coals or under an electric broiler, grilling is an extremely healthy low-fat cooking method. The vegetables are brushed lightly with the minimum of oil or butter. And because grilled food is cooked very quickly and is exposed to intense heat, it rapidly becomes crisp and the outer crust seals in the moistness and prevents it drying out. This helps retain the vegetables' intrinsic nutritional goodness, especially minerals and fat-soluble vitamins which can be diminished by boiling, frying or roasting.

Types of grills and fuels

There are many different types of outdoor grills, including braziers, rotisseries, hibachis, kettle grills and gas grills. Whichever grill you choose, it should be easy to use and to clean afterwards. If you have a gas grill on your deck, this is probably the most convenient. There is no need to gather up wood or spend time lighting charcoal; the grill heats up quickly, the amount of heat can be controlled, and it is easy to keep clean. However, the food will not have the authentic wonderful aroma and natural flavor that come from cooking over fruitwood or charcoal on to which some soaked hickory chips or sprigs of fresh rosemary, thyme or oregano have been thrown. Even just a little of one of these extra flavors will add to the overall taste of your food.

A broiler is the simplest way to grill vegetables and can produce delicious results if the vegetables are flavored with fruity olive oil, herbs, garlic, chiles or a spicy marinade. However, if you are addicted to the scent of woodsmoke and don't mind the extra work involved, then it is worth opting for the outdoor grill.

Grilling guidelines

1   For the best flavor, marinade vegetables for at least 30 minutes before grilling.
2   When removing the vegetables from the marinade, use paper towels to soak up any excess marinade.
3   If you don't use a marinade, brush the vegetables lightly with oil or some melted butter before grilling.
4   Always baste during cooking, especially when grilling over hot coals. This will help prevent the food drying out. You can use some oil or the left-over marinade.
5   Turn the vegetables frequently so that they cook evenly on all sides and a protective crust forms all over. Keep an eye on them so that they do not burn.

6 Start off by placing the vegetables close to the heat to sear them quickly and seal them, and then move them further away from the heat to finish cooking. You can do this by raising or lowering the grill rack or broiler tray.

7 Make sure the grill is really hot before putting any food on one of the racks. Preheat a broiler for at least 5 minutes.

8 The food is less likely to stick when cooked on a very hot grill. You can brush the grill rack lightly with a little oil to help prevent the vegetables sticking.

9 Keep an eye on the vegetables to insure that they do not get overcooked or become burnt offerings. Remember that grilled food cooks very quickly, literally in minutes, so don't go off to prepare another part of the meal and forget them.

10 The vegetables are cooked through when they are crisp and slightly charred on the outside and the inside is tender and moist. You can test them by piercing them with a sharp knife.

11 For the best results, grill your vegetables as and when you need them. If however, you are planning to add the grilled vegetables to a pie or pizza, cooking them in advance is fine, the additional cooking time will ensure they do not go soggy.

12 When grilling outdoors, be safety-conscious and keep a bowl or bottle of water handy to extinguish the fire if the food becomes engulfed by flames.

Equipment for grilling

Whatever equipment you choose to use, it is essential that it has a very long handle so that you can grill from a safe distance and minimize the risk of getting burnt. You will need the following items:

Tongs

These will enable you to handle and turn the food at arms' length. Because they have rounded ends, they will not pierce the vegetables which would allow the juicy moisture to escape.

Skewers

For kebobs, you can thread vegetables and cheeses on to metal or wooden skewers. Wooden ones should be soaked in water before using to prevent them burning over a hot fire.

Brushes

Use a long-handled basting brush for basting the vegetables during cooking. You will also need some smaller, softer-bristled brushes for brushing the food with oil or melted butter before cooking.

Gloves and apron

Wear a pair of sturdy oven gloves which come up over your wrists to protect you. If you value your clothing, cover up with an apron—grilled food can spit alarmingly at times.

Note: you will also need a long-handled fork, kitchen foil and paper towels. Throw-away foil trays can be useful for cooking delicate vegetables. Place them on the grill rack over the hot coals.

Marinades

These are flavored liquids in which the vegetables to be grilled are immersed before cooking. Marinading foods enhances their flavor and keeps them moist, especially when cooking over hot coals. Vegetables do not need to be marinated for a long time—30 minutes is usually sufficient. However, the longer that they are left in the marinade, the more flavor they absorb.

When marinading vegetables, make the marinade and transfer it to a large bowl. Add the vegetables, turning them in the marinade to cover all their surfaces. Cover the bowl and leave in the refrigerator until required, turning the vegetables occasionally so that the flavor of the marinade penetrates evenly. Drain the vegetables on paper towels before grilling. Don't throw the marinade away; you can use it for basting the vegetables while they cook, or as the base for a sauce. Most marinades will stay fresh in the refrigerator for two to three days.

Marinade ingredients

The base for most marinades is olive oil, which can be flavored with fruit juice (especially lime and lemon), garlic, herbs, spices, chiles, mustard, sun-dried tomatoes, fresh ginger root, honey, wine vinegar, and red or white wine.

Corn oil, peanut oil, walnut oil and hazelnut oil are all suitable. For an oriental flavor, try using sesame oil and flavoring it with soy sauce, ginger, star anise, lemon grass or cilantro.

Flavored butters

These can be made in advance and chilled until required—a small pat of melting flavored butter can really enhance a hot grilled vegetable. If you grill foods regularly, it is worthwhile making a larger quantity of flavored butter and storing it in the refrigerator or freezer. Chill the flavored butter, then roll it up into a sausage shape and wrap in kitchen foil. Just cut off thin slices when needed. Always use softened butter. Try adding finely chopped fresh herbs—such as, tarragon, parsley, cilantro, oregano, basil or mint—or the grated zest and juice of limes, lemons or oranges. For a red-hot flavor, blend finely chopped chiles into the butter. Alternatively, use crumbled blue cheese, shredded Swiss cheese or some chopped sun-dried tomatoes.For lime butter, mash ½ cup of butter with a little salt, grate the zest of 2 limes into the bowl. Squeeze in the juice from both limes, plus a little lime flesh and season to taste. Mix well. For garlic butter, mince 6 garlic cloves, finely chop 1 shallot and 1½ tablespoons of fresh parsley and mix with 1 cup sweet butter, cubed. Beat thoroughly. For ginger and mint butter beat ½ cup butter with 1 tablespoon of minced ginger root and 2 tablespoons of chopped fresh mint with seasoning to taste. For tarragon and lemon butter, beat together ½ cup butter with 3 tablespoons chopped fresh tarragon, 2 finely chopped shallots, the finely grated zest and juice of 1 lemon and add seasoning to taste.

Vegetables for grilling

Most vegetables are suitable for grilling, even salad leaves. It is important to prepare the vegetables so that they cook evenly right through to the center. They should be moist, tender and juicy on the inside, and crisp and just slightly charred on the outside. Here are some suggestions for vegetables that you can use.

Artichokes
Prepare in the usual way and cut them in half and brush with olive oil before grilling.

Asparagus
Trim the woody ends of asparagus stalks and brush with olive oil or melted butter before grilling.

Bell peppers
These grill more successfully than perhaps any other vegetables as grilling brings out their natural sweetness. They can be grilled whole, then placed in a plastic bag until cool enough to handle, and the skins peeled off and the cores and seeds removed. Alternatively, they can be cored, seeded and cut into chunks before threading onto skewers with other vegetables.

Broccoli
Small broccoli florets can be parboiled for 2–3 minutes, drained well, brushed with chili-flavored oil and then quickly seared on a hot grill, turning frequently.

Carrots
Use small tender carrots and dip in melted butter before grilling.

Chiles
Use fiery or mild chiles and grill whole over hot coals or open flames until charred and blistered all over. Be careful not to burn the flesh. Peel before eating.

Corn cobs
You can use large or baby ones. Shuck the corn, removing the outer husks and remove the silks before brushing with butter or oil. Grill for 5–10 minutes, until tender, turning frequently. You can cook them in their husks and then peel them and add melted butter before serving.

Eggplants
These can be grilled whole, cut in half or sliced; but do not peel them. A good way of cooking them is to cut them in half horizontally, score the flesh in a criss-cross pattern with a sharp knife, and then brush them all over with a good quality olive oil, especially the cut sides which will greedily soak up a lot of oil.

Fennel
Small fennel bulbs, either halved or sliced thickly, taste delicious grilled. Brush them with olive oil and turn once during cooking.

Garlic

Whole garlic bulbs can be grilled in their skins until tender, and then split open. The juicy, pungent flesh can be mashed up and spread on grilled ciabatta, used in salad dressings, or as a flavoring for butters and sauces.

Leeks

Small, slim leeks cook successfully on a grill. Wash them thoroughly before using to remove any dirt, and trim the ends. Brush with olive oil before grilling.

Mushrooms

Trim the stems level with the caps and thread on to kebob skewers, or wrap in kitchen foil with garlic-flavored butter and herbs. Or you can simply brush some large open-cap mushrooms with plenty of melted butter and a grinding of black pepper and grill until tender. Experiment with different types of wild mushrooms, such as cepes, morels, porcini and chanterelles, as well as the blander button mushrooms.

Onions

Red, white and pearl onions are all suitable for grilling. They can be left whole, brushed with olive oil, sprinkled with herbs and grilled in their skins to seal in maximum flavor; or they can be peeled and cut into quarters or large chunks before grilling.

Potatoes

Large potatoes can be wrapped in foil and then placed directly above the hot coals or cooked in the embers of the fire. Small unpeeled new potatoes can be parboiled for 5–10 minutes, then drained and brushed with olive oil, and put on the hot grill.

Pumpkin

Slices or large chunks of juicy pumpkin are excellent grilled. Remove the rind and brush with oil or butter before you start cooking. If wished, thread on to kebob skewers.

Red chicory

Trim the red chicory and cut into halves or quarters, brush with fruity extra-virgin olive oil and grill over hot coals until slightly charred but not burnt. Serve warm in a mustardy dressing.

Salad leaves

Many salad leaves and greens can be seared very quickly on the grill, and then tossed with grilled peppers, olives and garlic-flavored croutons in a French or vinaigrette dressing. You can of course use any other dressing if you prefer. Sliced avocado, grilled zucchini and eggplants are sometimes added. Choose strongly-flavored greens which will not disintegrate or go limp easily.

Scallions

Trimmed whole scallions can be brushed with olive oil and cooked on the grill, turning frequently, before adding to any kind of salad. In Mexican and Southwestern cookery, scallions are sometimes brushed with lime juice and salt before grilling.

Squash

Most squash are suitable for grilling, either whole, sliced or cut into chunks. Choose firm, unblemished squash, brush with oil and grill until slightly blackened.

Sweet potatoes

Grill whole, wrapped in kitchen foil, in the ashes of the fire, or cut into chunks, brush with oil or butter and grill until tender all the way through.

Tomatillos

The Mexican tomatillo, also called the Mexican green tomato or ground tomato, has a delicious distinctive flavor when grilled. Husk and wash the tomatillos, then grill until soft and blackened all over. The tomatillo ranges from cherry tomato to plum tomato in size. It is often sold when still pale green in color, at this stage it has a slightly acidic flavor. When the tomatillo ripens it turns bright yellow and becomes sweeter in flavor.

Tomatoes

You can use regular, cherry, plum or Roma tomatoes. Choose firm red ones and leave whole or cut in half. Grill until blackened and remove the skins before eating.

Zucchini

Use small zucchini; leave whole or cut into chunks and then brush with fruity olive oil before grilling until tender and well colored.

Grilled cheese

Some cheeses are much more suitable for grilling than others. The Greek haloumi cheese, firm individual goat's cheeses and camembert in its rind casing are especially suitable for grilling. There are other cheeses which are suitable for grilling, the more robust a cheese the better it will taste once grilled. Also, a firmer cheese will stand up to grilling better, but there are no hard and fast rules. If you want to try out a new cheese on the grill, you can always test grill a small portion of the new cheese before grilling a larger quantity if you achieve the results you want from the initial grilling. Do watch all cheeses carefully as you grill them, they will cook very quickly and can easily burn, if not watched. To tell if the grilled cheese is cooked, they should be crisp, golden and slightly charred on the outside, and melting seductively on the inside. Cooking times will vary for different cheeses but most will cook in 5–10 minutes.

MEDITERRANEAN VEGETABLE SALAD

Broiling the vegetables brings out their flavor to create a salad which evokes memories of freshly picked, sun-warmed Mediterranean zucchini, bell peppers and tomatoes.

2 small fennel bulbs
2 red onions
3 zucchini
4 tablespoons extra-virgin olive oil
I teaspoon finely grated lemon zest
I tablespoon chopped fresh thyme
I red or yellow bell pepper, cored, seeded and cut into wide strips
6 oz cherry tomatoes, halved

Dressing:
4 tablespoons extra-virgin olive oil
2 tablespoons lemon juice
pinch of sugar
I tablespoon chopped fresh oregano
salt and pepper

1 Cut the fennel bulbs and red onions into wedges, leaving the root ends intact to prevent them from falling apart during cooking. Halve the zucchini, then slice them thinly lengthwise.

2 Bring a large saucepan of water to a boil. Add the fennel and onions. When the water returns to a boil, cook the vegetables for 1 minute. Add the zucchini strips and cook for 1 minute more. Drain and refresh under cold running water, then drain thoroughly and set aside.

3 Combine the olive oil, lemon zest and thyme in a large bowl. Add all the vegetables and toss lightly to coat them in the flavored oil.

4 Line a broiler tray with kitchen foil. Spread the vegetable mixture evenly in a single layer in the tray. Cook under a preheated hot broiler for 15–20 minutes, turning frequently, until the vegetables are tender and patched with brown. Alternatively, grill over hot coals. Let the mixture cool.

5 Arrange the cooled vegetables on a serving plate. Make the dressing by whisking all the ingredients together in a small bowl. Alternatively place them in a screw-top jar, close the lid tightly and shake to combine. Pour the dressing over the vegetables and serve.

Serves 4
Preparation time: 25 minutes
Cooking time: about 20 minutes

SPANISH BELL PEPPER SALAD

2 green bell peppers
1 red bell pepper
1 yellow bell pepper
(or 1 extra red bell pepper)
2 garlic cloves, minced
2 small onions, thinly sliced into rings
2 tablespoons chopped fresh parsley
2 tablespoons black olives

Dressing:
3 tablespoons olive oil
2 teaspoons lemon juice
freshly ground black pepper

1 Place the bell peppers under a preheated moderately high broiler for about 15–20 minutes, turning them frequently, until their skins blacken. Cover with a damp cloth and leave them to cool. Peel.
2 Core and seed the bell peppers and cut them into thick slices. Toss with the minced garlic and the onion rings.
3 Heat the oil and lemon juice just to boiling point. Pour over the pepper mixture and mix well. Leave to cool. Season with pepper.
4 Stir in the parsley and olives and transfer to a serving dish.

Serves 4
Preparation time: 20 minutes
Cooking time: 20 minutes

BEAN SALAD WITH CHAR-GRILLED ONION

1⅓ cups dried cannellini beans, soaked overnight
2 large or 3 smaller red or mild white onions

Dressing:
⅝ cup light olive oil
5 tablespoons lemon juice
2 garlic cloves, minced
2 tablespoons finely chopped fresh parsley
pinch of mustard powder
pinch of sugar
salt and pepper

1 Drain the beans, then tip them into a saucepan. Cover with plenty of fresh water and bring to a boil. Boil rapidly for 10 minutes, then lower the heat, cover and simmer for 40–50 minutes, or until tender. Drain in a colander, rinse under cold running water, then drain again. Transfer to a bowl and set aside until cold.
2 Prepare the dressing by whisking all the ingredients together in a bowl or place them in a screw-top jar and shake until combined.
3 Peel the onions and cut into wedges, keeping the root ends intact. Place on a broiler rack and brush each wedge with a little dressing. Cook under a preheated moderately hot broiler for 8 minutes, until tender and beginning to char. Alternatively, grill over hot coals until just charred. Let cool.
4 Pile the onion wedges on top of the cold beans. Pour the remaining dressing over the salad and serve.

Serves 4
Preparation time: 20 minutes, plus overnight soaking
Cooking time: about 1 hour

SWEET POTATO AND CHILI SALAD

1½ pounds sweet potatoes, peeled
and sliced
3 large red chiles
6 tablespoons peanut oil, for frying
a handful of cilantro leaves, torn
coarse sea salt and pepper
small handful of lettuce leaves or arugula

Dressing:
1 teaspoon finely grated lime zest
2 tablespoons lime juice
4 tablespoons peanut oil
2 tablespoons sesame oil or 8 tablespoons
Ginger and Lime Dressing (see below)

1 Preheat the broiler to hot.
2 Boil the sweet potato slices in a large pan of boiling water for about 5 minutes. Drain well and then refresh under cold running water. Spread out on paper towels to dry.
3 Meanwhile, cook the chiles under the preheated hot broiler, turning frequently, until the skins are blistered and blackened all over. Let cool slightly, then carefully remove and discard the skin and seeds. Cut the flesh into thin strips and set aside.
4 Brush the sweet potato slices with the peanut oil. Spread out the sweet potato slices on a broiler tray lined with kitchen foil and place under a preheated moderate broiler and cook until crisp and lightly browned. Transfer to a large shallow serving bowl as they are done and add more to the pan as necessary.
5 To make the dressing, mix all the ingredients together in a small bowl until thoroughly blended or shake together in a screw-top jar.
6 Add the chili strips and cilantro to the salad bowl. Season with coarse sea salt and pepper to taste. Toss lightly to mix.
7 Just before serving, pour over the dressing and toss well. Serve with the lettuce or arugula

Serves 4
Preparation time: 15 minutes
Cooking time: about 20 minutes

GINGER AND LIME DRESSING

This dressing can be prepared ahead but the cilantro should be added just before serving.

2 teaspoons minced ginger root
1 garlic clove, minced
grated zest and juice of 2 limes
1 tablespoon clear honey
¼ cup peanut or grapeseed oil
2 tablespoons chopped fresh cilantro
salt and pepper

1 Combine the ginger and garlic together in a bowl. Add the lime zest to the bowl with the honey. Stir in salt and pepper to taste.
2 Add the lime juice to the bowl and beat well with a whisk or wooden spoon. Pour in the oil, whisking the dressing until well mixed. Just before using, stir in the chopped cilantro.

Makes about ⅝ cup
Preparation time: 10 minutes

PESTO AND BELL PEPPER SALAD

I red bell pepper
I yellow bell pepper
a bunch of mixed salad leaves, e.g. arugula,
Belgian endive, young spinach
½ cup black olives
I quantity Pesto Dressing (see below)
salt and pepper
sprigs of basil, to garnish

1 Cook the bell peppers under a preheated hot broiler for 15–20 minutes, turning occasionally, until the skins are blistered and blackened all over. Transfer the bell peppers to a bowl, cover with several layers of paper towels and set aside.

2 When cool enough to handle, rub off and discard the charred skin from the bell peppers. Slice the flesh into rings, discarding the seeds. Season with salt and pepper.

3 Arrange the salad leaves on a serving dish or individual plates. Pile the bell peppers on to the salad leaves, with the olives. Pour the dressing over the salad and toss lightly. Serve at once, garnished with sprigs of basil.

Serves 4
Preparation time: 20 minutes
Cooking time: 20 minutes

PESTO DRESSING

I oz basil leaves
3 tablespoons shredded Parmesan cheese
I tablespoon pine nuts
4 tablespoons white wine vinegar
I garlic clove, minced
freshly ground black pepper
½ cup extra-virgin olive oil

1 Combine the basil leaves, Parmesan, pine nuts, vinegar and garlic in a blender or food processor. Add pepper to taste. Process for a few seconds.

2 With the blender or food processor running, drizzle in the olive oil through the feeder tube until the mixture becomes thick and smooth. Pour into a bowl or jug and use as required.

Makes about I cup
Preparation time: 5 minutes

GRILLED BELL PEPPER AND ONION SALAD

3 onions
3 red bell peppers
3 yellow bell peppers
15 garlic cloves
1½ tablespoons fennel seeds
6 tablespoons olive oil
2 tablespoons balsamic vinegar
3 tablespoons coarsely chopped fresh parsley
salt and pepper

1 Peel the onions and cut into wedges, keeping the root ends intact so that the layers do not separate. Bring a saucepan of water to a boil, add the onions and cook for 1 minute, then drain well.

2 Halve the bell peppers lengthwise, cutting through the stems. Remove the seeds. Place the bell peppers, skin-side up, in a broiler tray. Add the onions and garlic cloves. Cook under a preheated hot broiler for about 10–15 minutes, turning occasionally, until the bell pepper skins are blistered and blackened all over. Turn the onions and garlic as necessary but let them char too. Alternatively, place them on a hot grill and cook until charred.

3 Transfer the bell peppers to a bowl, cover with several layers of paper towels and cool slightly. Rub off the charred bell pepper skin. Arrange the bell peppers, onions and 12 of the garlic cloves on individual plates.

4 In a small skillet, dry-roast the fennel seeds for a few minutes until they begin to pop and smell aromatic. Using a mortar and pestle, or a small strong bowl and the end of a rolling pin, roughly crush the fennel seeds with the 3 remaining broiled garlic cloves.

5 Whisk in the oil and vinegar, and season to taste.

6 Sprinkle the parsley over the salad and then spoon over the dressing. Serve this salad at room temperature.

Serves 6
Preparation time: 20 minutes
Cooking time: 11–16 minutes

VARIATION

BALSAMIC VINEGAR DRESSING

Use this alternative dressing if you prefer stronger flavors.

2 teaspoons balsamic vinegar
2 teaspoons whole-grain mustard
5 tablespoons extra-virgin olive oil
salt and pepper

Whisk together the vinegar, mustard, salt and pepper and then gradually whisk in the olive oil until blended.

Makes ½ cup
Preparation time: 5 minutes

CHAR-GRILLED PASTA SALAD

I large eggplant, sliced
I tablespoon salt
⅝ cup olive oil
2 cups dried penne rigate
6 tablespoons balsamic vinegar
I teaspoon Dijon mustard
2 celery stalks, chopped
½ cup drained canned red kidney beans
salt and pepper
I tablespoon chopped fresh parsley,
to garnish

1 Spread out the eggplant slices on some cookie sheets and sprinkle with the salt. Set aside for 15 minutes.

2 Meanwhile, bring at least 7½ cups water to a boil in a large saucepan. Add a dash of oil and a generous pinch of salt. Cook the pasta for 8–12 minutes, until just tender.

3 Drain the pasta and rinse under cold water in a colander. Drain again, transfer to a large salad bowl and set aside.

4 Rinse the eggplant slices under plenty of cold water, drain and pat dry with paper towels. Broil under a high heat for 10 minutes until crisp, turning once. Alternatively, grill over hot coals, turning once, for 5 minutes until colored. Slice each eggplant round in half. Set aside.

5 In a bowl, whisk the remaining olive oil with the vinegar and Dijon mustard. Add salt and pepper to taste. Add the dressing to the pasta and toss well. Fold in the celery and kidney beans, with the reserved eggplant slices. Scatter the parsley on top to garnish and serve at once.

Serves 4
Preparation time: 20 minutes, plus 15 minutes standing time
Cooking time: 12 minutes

GRILLED ASPARAGUS SALAD

Choose asparagus stalks of medium thickness for this salad. It is also delicious
with a dressing of garlic mayonnaise thinned to a pouring consistency with a little water.

1 pound asparagus
3 tablespoons olive oil
about 2 oz arugula
about 2 oz oak leaf lettuce
2 scallions, finely chopped
3–4 radishes, thinly sliced
6 tablespoons Tarragon and Lemon
Dressing (see below)
or Classic French Dressing (see page 21)
salt and pepper

To Garnish:
coarsely chopped fresh herbs,
e.g. tarragon, parsley, chervil, dill weed
thin strips of lemon zest

1 Trim the asparagus and use a potato peeler to peel about 2 inches off the base of each stalk. Arrange the asparagus in a single layer on a cookie sheet and brush with olive oil. Cook under a preheated hot broiler for about 7 minutes, turning frequently, until the asparagus stalks are just tender when pierced with the point of a sharp knife and lightly patched with brown. Sprinkle with salt and pepper and leave to cool. Alternatively, grill over moderately hot coals for 5 minutes, turning frequently.

2 Arrange the arugula and lettuce on a serving platter or on 4 individual plates. Scatter with scallions and radishes. Season with salt and pepper and leave to cool.

3 Arrange the asparagus beside the salad leaves and drizzle with the dressing. Garnish with a sprinkling of coarsely chopped fresh herbs and thin strips of lemon zest.

Serves 4
Preparation time: 15 minutes
Cooking time: about 7 minutes

TARRAGON AND LEMON DRESSING

2 tablespoons tarragon vinegar
1 teaspoon finely grated lemon zest
¼ teaspoon Dijon mustard
pinch of sugar
1 tablespoon chopped fresh tarragon
5 tablespoons olive oil or grapeseed oil
salt and pepper

1 Combine the vinegar, lemon zest, mustard, sugar and tarragon in a small bowl. Add salt and pepper to taste. Stir to mix, then gradually whisk in the oil.

2 Alternatively, mix all the ingredients in a screw-top jar, close the lid tightly and shake well to combine.

Makes about ¼ cup
Preparation time: 5 minutes

GRILLED EGGPLANT SALAD

2 eggplants, trimmed
2 teaspoons salt
I quantity Classic French Dressing (see below)
3 scallions, finely chopped
sprigs of fresh herbs, e.g. thyme, dill weed, parsley, cilantro, basil, chives
freshly ground black pepper

I Cut the eggplants into slices about ½ inch thick. Arrange in a colander and sprinkle with the salt. Set the colander over a bowl or in the sink and leave for 30–40 minutes to allow the bitter juices from the eggplants to run out.

2 Rinse the eggplant slices under cold running water, drain and pat dry with paper towels. Arrange in a single layer on a cookie sheet. Brush with a little of the dressing. Cook under a preheated hot broiler for about 5 minutes, turning once, until browned on both sides, then transfer to a shallow serving bowl. Alternatively, grill over moderately hot coals, turning once, until colored.

3 Add the scallions to the bowl and season with black pepper. Spoon over the remaining dressing and toss lightly. Leave until cold, then sprinkle over the herbs before serving.

Serves 6
Preparation time: 15 minutes, plus standing time
Cooking time: 5 minutes

CLASSIC FRENCH DRESSING

This basic recipe for French Dressing can easily be adapted by adding ingredients such as chopped fresh herbs, minced onion, chopped capers or finely grated lemon or orange zest.

2 tablespoons red or white wine vinegar
I–2 garlic cloves, minced
2 teaspoons Dijon mustard
¼ teaspoon sugar
6 tablespoons olive oil
salt and pepper

I Combine the vinegar, garlic, mustard and sugar in a small bowl. Add salt and pepper and stir well.

2 Gradually whisk in the olive oil, taste and add more salt and pepper if necessary.

3 Alternatively, put all the ingredients in a screw-top jar, close the lid tightly and shake well until combined. Use as required.

Makes about ⅝ cup
Preparation time: 5 minutes

GRILLED VEGETABLE AND BREAD SALAD

1 large eggplant, cubed
4 zucchini, cubed
2 red bell peppers, cored,
seeded and sliced
4 whole peeled garlic cloves
extra-virgin olive oil
4 firm ripe tomatoes, diced
4 cups day-old-bread, diced
2 tablespoons boiling water
4 tablespoons fresh basil leaves

Dressing:
9 tablespoons extra-virgin olive oil
2 tablespoons red wine vinegar
pinch of sugar
3 tablespoons boiling water
salt and pepper

1 Toss the eggplant, zucchini, bell peppers and garlic cloves in about 4 tablespoons of olive oil and place in a broiler tray lined with kitchen foil. Place under a preheated broiler for 15–20 minutes, turning frequently until the vegetables are tender and slightly charred. Or grill over moderately hot coals, turning once, until lightly browned.

2 Transfer the vegetables to a bowl and stir in the tomatoes with a little extra oil if necessary. Whisk the dressing ingredients together, except for the water. Stir 3 tablespoons of the dressing into the vegetables and leave to cool.

3 Place the bread in a bowl. Add the boiling water to the remaining dressing and stir into the bread, then leave to soak for 10 minutes. Just before serving, add the bread to the vegetables with the basil and season to taste. Transfer to a serving dish and serve at room temperature.

Serves 6
Preparation time: 25 minutes, plus cooling time
Cooking time: 15–20 minutes

WHOLE BAKED CORN WITH SKORTHALIA

Cobs of tender young corn, preferably freshly picked, are delicious when spread with this rich garlic sauce.

4 whole corn cobs, with husks

Skorthalia:
1 cup fresh white breadcrumbs
½ cup ground almonds
4 garlic cloves, minced
2 tablespoons lemon juice
⅝ cup extra-virgin olive oil
salt and pepper

1 To make the skorthalia, place the breadcrumbs in a bowl and cover with water. Soak for 5 minutes, then squeeze out the excess liquid and place the crumbs in a blender or food processor. Add the ground almonds, garlic and 1 tablespoon of the lemon juice. Process until mixed. With the motor running, gradually add the olive oil in a thin steady stream until the mixture resembles mayonnaise. Add more lemon juice and salt and pepper to taste.
2 Pull down the outer leaves of the corn husks and remove the inner silks. Pull the leaves back over the corn kernels. Place on a grill over hot coals. Cook for about 30–40 minutes until the kernels are juicy and easily come away from the cob.
3 To serve, pull back the leaves of the corn cobs and spread with the skorthalia.

Serves 4
Preparation time: 15 minutes
Cooking time: 30–40 minutes

24

BAKED STUFFED SQUASH

Melting buttery baby squash with couscous and fudgy grilled dates.

a generous pinch of saffron threads
2¼ cups boiling water
1⅓ cups quick-cooking couscous
2 large eggplants
2 tablespoons salt
6 tablespoons olive oil
½ teaspoon ground cinnamon
1 cup pecan nuts, toasted and chopped
2 small acorn squash, cut in half lengthwise, seeds removed
2 tablespoons butter
12 medjool dates, threaded on 4 small skewers (soaked 30 minutes in water if wooden)
salt and pepper

1 Infuse the saffron for 10 minutes in the boiling water in a large heatproof bowl. Add the couscous, stir and leave to stand for 6–8 minutes, until it swells and absorbs all the water. Fluff up the grains with a fork and set aside.

2 Slice the eggplants lengthwise into ½-inch slices. Place in layers in a colander and sprinkle each layer with salt. Leave to stand for 30 minutes, then rinse well under cold running water. Drain and pat dry with paper towels.

3 Using 3 tablespoons of the olive oil, brush the eggplant slices on both sides. Cook under a preheated broiler (or on the barbecue grill) for 5–6 minutes on each side, until tender. Cool slightly, cut the slices into ½-inch strips, and add to the couscous. Add the cinnamon, pecans and seasoning. Toss well.

4 Brush the squash with the remaining oil and fill with the couscous mixture. Dot with the butter. Wrap each half in a double thickness of kitchen foil and place in the embers of the barbecue for 30 minutes, or until the flesh is tender.

5 Place the dates on the grill for 3–4 minutes, until golden. Turn frequently.

6 To serve, unwrap each squash and serve with a date kebob.

Serves 4
Preparation time: 1 hour
Cooking time: about 30 minutes

GRILLED RED CHICORY WITH PEARS AND ROQUEFORT

The slight bitterness of the red chicory combines well with citrus-sweet baked pears and creamy sharp cheese to make a dish which is equally suitable as an unusual appetizer or as an ending to a rich meal. Sadly the ruby red color of the red chicory is somewhat lost in cooking but the flavor is delicious none the less.

4 ripe pears
finely grated zest and juice of 2 oranges
4 tablespoons clear honey
4 small red chicory
I tablespoon walnut oil
I cup crumbled Roquefort or other blue cheese
freshly ground black pepper

I Cut each pear into quarters lengthwise and remove the cores. Place the pears in a single layer on a large sheet of double kitchen foil, turning up the edges slightly.

2 Mix the orange zest and juice and honey in a jug. Pour over the pears.

3 Bring up the edges of the kitchen foil and press together to seal. Place the parcel on a grill over moderately hot coals and cook for about 15–20 minutes, or until the pears are tender.

4 About 6 minutes before the pears are ready, cook the red chicory. Cut each one into quarters, brush with the walnut oil and cook on the grill for 2–3 minutes on each side.

5 To serve, divide the pears and their cooking juices between 4 plates. Add 4 red chicory quarters to each portion, then sprinkle with the crumbled Roquefort and a little pepper.

Serves 4
Preparation time: 5 minutes
Cooking time: 15–20 minutes

STUFFED MINI BELL PEPPERS WITH TOMATO SAUCE

Miniature bell peppers, stuffed with a creamy minted cheese, are delicious with plain grilled chicken or as an appetizer.

8 mini bell peppers
Greek yogurt, to serve

Stuffing:
¼ pound soft fresh goat's cheese
⅓ cup ricotta
1½ tablespoons chopped fresh mint
1 red or green chili, seeded and finely chopped (optional)
salt and pepper

Tomato Sauce:
1 tablespoon olive oil
1 onion, finely chopped
1 garlic clove, minced
1½ cups canned tomatoes
1 tablespoon chopped fresh parsley
1 tablespoon chopped fresh oregano

1 To make the tomato sauce, heat the oil in a saucepan, add the onion and the garlic and cook for 5 minutes, until softened but not colored. Stir in the canned tomatoes and herbs and simmer gently for 10 minutes. Strain the sauce through a strainer set over a clean pan. Set aside.

2 To make the stuffing, combine the goat's cheese, ricotta and mint in a bowl. Stir in the chili, if using, and season to taste.

3 Make a small slit in the side of each bell pepper, carefully scrape out the seeds and core with a teaspoon, keeping the shells intact. Half-fill each pepper with stuffing—do not be tempted to fill them completely, or they may burst during cooking.

4 Cook the filled peppers on an oiled grill over moderately hot coals for about 10–15 minutes, turning occasionally, until softened. Meanwhile, reheat the tomato sauce by placing the pan at the edge of the barbecue grill.

5 Place 2 of the filled peppers on each plate and serve with the tomato sauce and a generous spoonful of Greek yogurt, if liked.

Serves 4
Preparation time: 20 minutes
Cooking time: 10–15 minutes

HOT ASPARAGUS WITH BALSAMIC AND TOMATO DRESSING

Asparagus is perfect for the barbecue as it cooks quickly and easily. Serve this as a appetizer, with lots of warm bread to mop up the juices, while you prepare the main course.

2 tablespoons balsamic vinegar
1–2 garlic cloves, minced
¾ pound tomatoes, skinned, seeded and chopped
7 tablespoons olive oil
1 pound young asparagus stalks
⅛ cup pine nuts, toasted
3 tablespoons Parmesan cheese, shaved into thin slivers
sea salt flakes and pepper

1 Place the vinegar, garlic, chopped tomatoes and 5 tablespoons of the olive oil in a small bowl. Mix well to combine and set aside.
2 Trim the asparagus stalks to remove any tough fibrous ends. Brush them with the remaining olive oil and cook on an oiled grill over moderately hot coals for about 5–6 minutes, until tender.
3 Divide the grilled asparagus between 4 warmed serving plates. Spoon over the balsamic vinegar and tomato dressing, top with the toasted pine nuts and Parmesan slivers and sprinkle with the sea salt flakes and pepper. Serve at once.

Serves 4
Preparation time: 15 minutes
Cooking time: 5–6 minutes

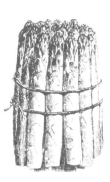

BROILED CAPPELLINI SALSA

oil (see method)
10 oz dried cappellini (angel hair pasta)
1 cup shreddeded mozzarella
salt and pepper
1 tablespoon chopped fresh parsley,
to garnish

Salsa:
1 onion, chopped finely
1 green bell pepper, cored,
seeded and diced
1 teaspoon hot chili sauce
1 pound plum tomatoes, chopped

1 Make the salsa. Place the onion, bell pepper, chili sauce and tomatoes in a bowl, mix well, then set aside for about 10 minutes.
2 Meanwhile, bring at least 7½ cups of water to a boil in a large saucepan. Add a dash of oil and a generous pinch of salt. Cook the pasta for 5–7 minutes, until just tender.
3 Drain the pasta and return it to the clean pan. Add the salsa and toss well. Add salt and pepper to taste.
4 Transfer the mixture to a lightly greased 2-pint ovenproof dish. Sprinkle over the mozzarella and place under a preheated hot broiler for about 15 minutes, or until the topping is golden.
5 Serve at once, garnished with the parsley.

Serves 4
Preparation time: 10 minutes, plus 10 minutes marinading time
Cooking time: 22 minutes

GREEN CHILI SALSA

If you prefer a slightly hotter salsa use this recipe instead of the one above.

1 pound large ripe tomatoes, skinned
and chopped
2 fresh green chiles, seeded
and finely chopped
1 small red onion, finely chopped
pinch of sugar
few sprigs fresh cilantro, chopped
salt and freshly ground black pepper

1 Put the tomatoes, chiles and onion in a bowl with the sugar. Season to taste and stir in the cilantro.

Makes 1½ cups
Preparation time: 6–8 minutes

GRILLED SWEET POTATO WITH AIOLI

Aioli, or garlic mayonnaise, is served here with delicious nutty sweet potatoes.
You could also add 2 tablespoons chopped fresh mixed herbs to the aioli.

I pound sweet potatoes, scrubbed
4 tablespoons olive oil
salt and pepper

Aioli:
4–6 garlic cloves, minced
2 egg yolks
juice of ½ lemon, plus extra, to taste
I ¼ cups extra-virgin olive oil

I To make the aioli, place the garlic and egg yolks in a blender or food processor, add the lemon juice and process briefly to mix. With the motor running, gradually add the olive oil in a thin steady stream until the mixture forms a thick cream. Add salt and pepper to taste and stir in more lemon juice if liked. Scrape the aioli into a bowl and set aside.

2 To prepare the sweet potatoes, cut each potato into ¼-inch slices, brush with the olive oil and place on an oiled grill over moderately hot coals. Grill for about 5 minutes on each side until tender. Serve hot with the aioli.

Serves 4
Preparation time: 15 minutes
Cooking time: 10 minutes

GRILLED MARINADED VEGETABLES

2 red onions
2 yellow bell peppers
2 green bell peppers
I large eggplant
about I cup olive oil
2 garlic cloves, minced
2 tablespoons chopped fresh parsley
8 plum tomatoes, halved
3 firm zucchini, halved lengthwise
12 large firm mushrooms, trimmed
salt and freshly ground black pepper

1 Remove the outer skin from the onions, leaving the point intact. Cut each onion in half horizontally. Trim the stalk end of each bell pepper neatly. Cut the eggplant in half lengthwise. Score the flesh, without cutting through the skin, and sprinkle generously with salt. Leave to drain upside down on a wire rack for 30 minutes.
2 Mix the olive oil, garlic and parsley together in a large bowl, and add all the vegetables. Season with salt and pepper. Set aside to marinade for 1 hour.
3 Remove the vegetables from the marinade. Place them all on a grill rack over moderately hot coals. Grill, turning occasionally for 5–10 minutes, until the skins are slightly charred and the vegetables are tender. Baste frequently with the marinade. Transfer the grilled vegetables to a serving plate.

Serves 6–8
Preparation time: 15 minutes, plus marinading time
Cooking time: 5–10 minutes

MIXED GRILLED VEGETABLES WITH OLIVE AND WALNUT PASTE

Choose a selection of vegetables in season to serve with this rich green olive and walnut paste.
Asparagus and fennel are also excellent when barbecued.

1 large eggplant
2 red bell peppers
2 yellow bell peppers
2 zucchini
8 baby leeks
6 tablespoons olive oil
4 large slices crusty country bread
salt and pepper

Olive and Walnut Paste:
⅓ cup pitted green olives
½ cup walnut pieces
¼ cup bottled pickled walnuts, drained
2 garlic cloves, minced
a small bunch of fresh parsley
½ cup extra-virgin olive oil

1 To make the olive and walnut paste, place the olives, fresh and pickled walnuts, garlic and parsley in a blender or food processor and process until finely chopped. Gradually add the olive oil through the feeder tube until the mixture forms a stiff paste. Scrape into a bowl and season with salt and pepper.

2 Cut the eggplant into ½-inch thick slices. Place in layers in a colander set over a plate to catch the juices. Sprinkle each layer with salt. Leave to stand for 30 minutes, then rinse under cold running water, drain well and pat dry with paper towels.

3 Cut the bell peppers in half. Remove the seeds but leave the stalks on. Slice the zucchini lengthwise. Rinse the leeks well to remove any dirt.

4 Brush the eggplants, bell peppers, zucchini and leeks with the olive oil. Place on an oiled grill over moderately hot coals. Cook the eggplants and peppers for 6–8 minutes, the zucchini and leeks for 3 minutes, turning frequently, until tender. Brush the bread with any remaining olive oil and grill until golden. Spread the toast with the olive and walnut paste and top with the vegetables.

Serves 4
Preparation time: 1 hour
Cooking time: 10 minutes

GLAZED MUSHROOM AND BEAN CURD KEBOBS

10 oz bean curd, evenly cubed
16 large button mushrooms, wiped
2 tablespoons sesame oil
6 tablespoons Tamari soy sauce
4 tablespoons red wine vinegar
2 teaspoons shredded ginger root
2 garlic cloves, minced
2 tablespoons clear honey
4 tablespoons water

Chili Sauce:
1 tablespoon light brown sugar
2 tablespoons soy sauce
1 tablespoon lime juice
1 red chili, deseeded and chopped

Peanut Sauce:
1 tablespoon corn oil
1 garlic clove, minced
1 red chili, seeded and finely chopped
4 tablespoons crunchy peanut butter
1 tablespoon dark soy sauce
1 tablespoon lime juice
½ oz creamed coconut

To Garnish (optional):
rice cubes
shredded cucumber
sprigs of cilantro

1 Thread the bean curd and mushrooms alternately on to 8 pre-soaked bamboo skewers Combine the flavorings, honey and water in a small saucepan and bring to a boil. Boil rapidly until the sauce is thick and glossy and reduced by half. Leave to cool slightly.

2 To make the chili sauce, combine all the ingredients in a small saucepan and heat, stirring occasionally, until the sugar dissolves.

3 Make the peanut sauce. Heat the oil in a small saucepan and gently fry the garlic and chili for 3 minutes. Gradually stir in the remaining ingredients. Bring slowly to a boil, stirring constantly, and add enough boiling water to make a smooth pouring sauce. Cover the surface with plastic wrap and keep warm.

4 Transfer the kebobs to a hot grill, brush all over with the glaze and cook for 8–10 minutes over moderately hot coals, turning and basting frequently, until golden and tender. Serve the kebobs hot with the 2 sauces, to dip. Accompany with rice cubes and shredded cucumber. Garnish with sprigs of cilantro, if liked.

Serves 4 as an appetizer
Preparation time: 30 minutes, plus making chili sauce
Cooking time: 8–10 minutes

MIXED VEGETABLE KEBOBS

2 medium zucchini
salt
4 pearl onions or shallots, peeled
8 small button mushrooms, trimmed
4 medium tomatoes, halved,
or 8 cherry tomatoes
I red bell pepper, cored, seeded and cut
into 2-inch squares
I2 small bay leaves

Marinade:
4 tablespoons corn oil
I tablespoon red wine vinegar
I tablespoon lemon juice
I garlic clove, minced
2 tablespoons chopped fresh mint
freshly ground black pepper
½ teaspoon mustard power

Rice:
I cup brown rice
2½ cups chicken broth
salt
I teaspoon ground coriander
2 tablespoons chopped cilantro
leaves or parsley

1 Blanch the zucchini and onions in boiling, salted water for 2 minutes. Drain.

2 Trim the zucchini and cut them into 1½-inch slices.

3 Thread all the vegetables and the bay leaves on to 4 greased skewers and lay them in a shallow dish.

4 Mix together all the marinade ingredients and pour over the kebobs. Turn in the marinade to coat the vegetables thoroughly. Cover and set aside at room temperature for about 2 hours.

5 Put the rice in a pan with the broth, salt and ground coriander. Bring to a boil, stir well, cover and simmer for 45 minutes.

6 Drain the kebobs from the marinade. Place under a preheated moderate broiler and cook for 8 minutes, turning frequently and brushing with the remaining marinade. Alternatively, place over hot coals and grill for 4–5 minutes.

7 Stir the chopped cilantro into the rice and spoon into a heated serving dish. Arrange the kebobs on top and serve at once. Serve with a green salad.

Serves 4

Preparation time: 25 minutes, plus 2 hours marinading
Cooking time: 45 minutes

BROILED FALL VEGETABLES WITH GARLIC SAUCE

Broiling vegetables draws out their natural sweetness and intense flavor. It is important to cut the vegetables into similar-sized pieces so that they cook evenly.

I large bulb garlic
2 large onions, cut into wedges
8 small carrots, quartered
8 small parsnips
12 small potatoes, halved if large
2 fennel bulbs, sliced thickly
4 sprigs rosemary
4 sprigs thyme
6 tablespoons extra-virgin olive oil

Garlic Sauce:
I large slice day-old bread
4 tablespoons milk
¼ cup extra-virgin olive oil
salt and pepper

1 Blanch the whole bulb of garlic in boiling water for 5 minutes. Drain and pat dry on paper towels.

2 Put all the vegetables and herbs in a broiler tray lined with kitchen foil, placing the garlic in the middle. Season well and stir in the oil to coat the vegetables. Cook under a preheated broiler for 20–30 minutes, turning frequently so that the vegetables cook evenly. They should be slightly charred but not burnt.

3 Remove the garlic. Carefully peel and discard the skin and mash the garlic flesh with a fork.

4 To make the garlic sauce, put the bread in a bowl, add the milk and soak for 5 minutes.

5 Place the bread and garlic flesh in a blender and process to form a smooth paste. Gradually blend in the oil, a little at a time, until evenly combined and season to taste.

6 Serve the broiled vegetables accompanied by the garlic sauce for dipping.

Serves 4–6
Preparation time: 25 minutes
Cooking time: 20–30 minutes

BOCCONCINI AND CHERRY TOMATO KEBOBS

2 thick slices of focaccia bread
8 cherry tomatoes
8 sun-dried tomatoes in oil
½ pound mini mozzarella cheeses
(bocconcini)

Marinade:
1 garlic clove
juice of 1 lemon
salt
2 teaspoons Pesto Sauce (see below)
6 tablespoons olive oil

1 To make the marinade, mince the garlic and stir with the lemon juice and salt into the pesto sauce. Whisk in the olive oil.
2 Cut the focaccia bread into chunks and toss briefly in the marinade, then remove. Add the cherry tomatoes, sun-dried tomatoes and mozzarella and leave for 30 minutes.
3 Thread onto kebob sticks, starting and finishing with a cube of bread. Grill over hot coals for 2–3 minutes each side, basting with the marinade until the bread is crisp and the cheese is just beginning to melt.

Serves 4
Preparation time: 15 minutes, plus 30 minutes marinading
Cooking time: 2–3 minutes

PESTO SAUCE

1 garlic clove, minced
¼ cup pine nuts
1 oz basil leaves
¼ cup extra-virgin olive oil
2 tablespoons freshly shredded Parmesan
cheese
salt and pepper

Place the garlic, pine nuts and basil in a blender and process until fairly smooth (or grind using a pestle and mortar). Gradually beat in the oil, then stir in the cheese and adjust the seasoning to taste.

Makes about ⅝ cup
Preparation time: 10 minutes

VARIATION
RED PESTO SAUCE

Add ⅛ cup sliced sun-dried tomatoes in oil to the garlic, pine nuts and basil. You can substitute half the oil from the sun-dried tomatoes for half the olive oil for an even stronger flavor.

POLENTA AND VEGETABLE KEBOBS

I red bell pepper
4 tablespoons olive oil
½ pound mushrooms, quartered
2 red onions, cut into small wedges
¼ pound baby zucchini, cut in half
lengthwise
¼ lb baby carrots
¼ pound French beans, trimmed
¼ pound broccoli, cut into florets
6¼ cups water
1⅔ cups polenta
⅓ cup Parmesan cheese, shredded, plus
extra for sprinkling
2 garlic cloves, minced
8 ripe plum tomatoes,
cut in half lengthwise
½ cup black olives
salt and pepper

1 Place the red bell pepper under a preheated broiler for 10 minutes until blistered and charred. Place in a plastic bag, close tightly and set aside to cool. Peel off the charred skin, cut the bell pepper in half and remove the seeds. Cut the flesh into 1-inch wide strips.
2 Heat half the oil in a skillet, add the mushrooms and onions, cover and cook for 2–3 minutes. Remove and drain on paper towels.
3 Blanch the remaining vegetables in separate saucepans of boiling salted water until crisp and tender. Drain, refresh under cold running water and drain well.
4 Bring the measured water to a boil in a large saucepan. Add a pinch of salt, then pour in the polenta in a thin steady stream, stirring all the time. Reduce the heat and continue to stir the mixture (beating as it thickens) for about 20 minutes until it leaves the sides of the pan clean. Remove from the heat and stir in the Parmesan cheese. Pour the polenta out into a mound on a board, leave to cool, then cut into 1-inch cubes.
5 Thread the cubes of polenta on to skewers, alternating with the red onions, mushrooms, squares of red bell pepper, thickly sliced zucchini and blanched carrots. Brush with olive oil. Grill for about 5–6 minutes on each side, over moderately hot coals, until the vegetables are tender and the polenta cubes are golden.
6 Meanwhile, mix the remaining olive oil with the mixed garlic and brush over the tomatoes. Season to taste and cook on a hot grill, cut-side down, for 5–6 minutes, turning once. Serve with the kebobs, garnished with black olives and sprinkled with the remaining Parmesan cheese.

Serves 6-8
Preparation time: 1 hour 10 minutes
Cooking time: 5–6 minutes

GRILLED BELL PEPPER AND ONION PIE

Yeast Pie Crust:
I cup bread flour
I cup strong whole-wheat flour
I teaspoon fast-rising active dried yeast
I teaspoon salt
⅝ cup hand-hot water
I tablespoon olive oil

Topping:
¾ cup canned chopped tomatoes
I tablespoon tomato paste
2 teaspoons dried oregano
I onion, cut into wedges
2 red bell peppers, cored, seeded and cut into strips
2 yellow bell peppers, cored, seeded and cut into strips
2 tablespoons olive oil
salt and pepper

1 For the pie crust, mix the flours, yeast and salt in a bowl. Add the water and oil and mix quickly to a soft dough. Turn the dough out on to a lightly floured surface and knead for 5 minutes. Place the dough in a large oiled plastic bag, tie the top loosely and leave to rise for 30 minutes.

2 Make the topping. Combine the chopped tomatoes and tomato paste in a saucepan. Add 1 teaspoon of the oregano, with salt and pepper to taste. Bring to a boil, stirring, then lower the heat and simmer for about 5 minutes, until thickened. Leave to cool.

3 Place the onion wedges and bell peppers on a sheet of oiled kitchen foil on a broiler tray. Brush with oil, sprinkle with salt and pepper. Cook under a preheated hot broiler for about 10 minutes, turning frequently, until softened and slightly charred. Alternatively, grill over hot coals.

4 Roll out the dough on a lightly floured surface to a 10-inch square and place on a greased cookie sheet. Fold up the edges of the dough to form a rim. Spread with the tomato topping, then arrange the char-grilled peppers and onion over the top. Sprinkle with the remaining oregano.

5 Bake the pie in a preheated oven at 425°F for 20–25 minutes, until the pie shell is crisp and golden brown. Serve warm.

Serves 4–6
Preparation time: 45 minutes
Cooking time: 20–25 minutes
Oven temperature: 425°F

BROILED MEDITERRANEAN VEGETABLE SOUP

1 large onion, halved but not peeled
4 garlic cloves
4 ripe but firm tomatoes
2 eggplants, total weight about 1½ pounds, halved lengthwise
2 red bell peppers, halved
3 tablespoons extra-virgin olive oil, plus extra for brushing
5 sprigs of thyme
1 fresh bay leaf, torn
4–5 halves of sun-dried tomatoes, chopped
6¼ cups good chicken or vegetable broth
6 large basil leaves, torn
lemon juice, to taste
salt and pepper

1 Cook the onion, garlic, tomatoes, eggplants and bell peppers under a preheated hot broiler until softened. Cool, peel the onion, garlic and tomatoes. Remove the charred patches from the eggplants and bell peppers, discard pepper cores and seeds. Coarsely chop them all. 2 Gently heat the olive oil with the thyme and bay leaf for a few minutes. Add the chopped vegetables, sun-dried tomatoes and broth. Bring to a boil, cover and simmer gently for 20 minutes. Add the basil and simmer for a further 5 minutes. Cool slightly, then puree briefly in a blender or food processor. Return to the pan, add lemon juice to taste. Reheat—the soup is best eaten warm, not hot.

Serves 4–6

Preparation time: 20 minutes
Cooking time: 20 minutes
Oven temperature: 400°F

EGGPLANT, TOMATO AND HALOUMI CHEESE PIE

½ pound puff pastry, thawed if frozen
beaten egg or milk, to glaze
1 tablespoon sun-dried tomato paste
¾ pound eggplants, sliced
2 tablespoons olive oil
5 ripe tomatoes, sliced
¼ pound haloumi cheese, sliced thinly
2 teaspoons chopped fresh oregano
½ cup green olives, pitted and halved
salt and pepper

1 Roll out the dough on a floured surface to a 10-inch square. Place on a greased cookie sheet. Using a knife, make 2 "L"-shaped cuts in the dough, 1 inch from the edges; leave the opposite corners uncut. 2 Brush the dough edges with water. Lift up one cut corner and draw it across to the opposite cut side. Repeat with the other cut side to form a pie shell. Brush the edges with beaten egg or milk. Prick the base with a fork. Spread the tomato paste over the base. 3 Place the eggplant on a broiler tray and brush both sides with oil. Cook under a preheated broiler until both sides are lightly browned. 4 Arrange the eggplant, tomatoes and cheese in the pie shell. Scatter with oregano and olives, add seasoning to taste. Bake in a preheated oven at 400°F for 25 minutes, until golden and tender. Serve warm.

Serves 4

Preparation time: 20 minutes
Cooking time: 25 minutes
Oven temperature: 400°F

MEDITERRANEAN VEGETABLE PARCEL

4½ cups self-rising flour
1 teaspoon salt
¾ cup vegetable suet
⅝ cup natural yogurt
1 cup milk

Filling:
2 eggplants
2 tablespoons extra-virgin olive oil
2 red bell peppers, cored, seeded and quartered
4 firm ripe tomatoes, sliced
12 large basil leaves
6 oz mozzarella cheese, sliced thinly
beaten egg or milk to glaze

1 Sift the flour and salt into a large bowl, stir in the suet and then gradually work in the yogurt and milk to form a stiff dough. Knead lightly until smooth, place in a plastic bag and leave to rest.
2 Thinly slice the eggplants lengthwise, brush with a little oil and cook under a hot broiler for 5–6 minutes on each side until golden and tender. Broil the bell pepper quarters for 6–8 minutes until charred and tender, wrap in a plastic bag and leave until cool enough to handle. Peel off the skin.
3 Roll out the dough on a lightly floured surface to a 14-inch square. Arrange the eggplants, bell peppers, tomatoes, basil and cheese in layers, diagonally in the center of the square, forming an 8-inch square shape.
4 Dampen the edges of the dough with a little water and draw up the 4 corners, pressing together in the middle to seal in the filling.
5 Transfer the parcel to an oiled cookie sheet, brush with egg glaze and bake in a preheated oven at 400°F for 30 minutes. Lower the temperature to 350°F, and bake for a further 15 minutes until puffed up and golden. Rest for 5 minutes and serve hot with mushroom gravy and a green salad.

Serves 4
Preparation time: 40 minutes, plus making mushroom gravy
Cooking time: 1 hour
Oven temperature: 400°F, then 350°F

MOZZARELLA AND TOMATO TOASTS

4 thick slices farmhouse country bread
4 tomatoes, skinned and sliced
salt and freshly ground black pepper
1 green or yellow bell pepper, cored,
seeded and sliced
3 oz mozzarella cheese, thinly sliced
1 teaspoon dried mixed herbs
4–8 small black olives
sprigs of parsley, to garnish

1 Place the bread under a preheated hot broiler and toast until golden on one side.
2 Turn the bread slices over and cover with the tomatoes, adding salt and pepper to taste. Top with the bell pepper slices and mozzarella cheese. Sprinkle over the herbs, place under a preheated moderate broiler and toast for about 10 minutes, until cooked through and bubbling.
3 Serve hot, topped with the black olives and garnished with sprigs of parsley.

Serves 4
Preparation time: 10 minutes
Cooking time: 15 minutes

MUSHROOMS ON TOAST

Mushrooms on Toast makes an ideal snack or light supper dish.

14 oz button mushrooms, rinsed,
trimmed and sliced
1 tablespoon lemon juice
1 tablespoon butter
½ tablespoon chopped fresh basil
2 tablespoons chopped fresh parsley
2 tablespoons heavy cream
2 tablespoons olive oil
4 slices white bread
2 oz mild cheese, sliced
salt and freshly ground black pepper

1 Sprinkle the mushrooms with the lemon juice and leave to stand for 5 minutes.
2 Melt the butter in a saucepan. Add the mushrooms and cook, over a moderate heat, for 2 minutes. Add the basil, parsley, cream, and salt and pepper to taste. Reduce the heat and simmer gently for about 7 minutes, or until the mushrooms are cooked.
3 Meanwhile, heat the oil in a skillet, add the bread and fry until golden brown on both sides, then drain on paper towels. Divide the mushrooms equally between the slices of bread and top with the cheese. Place under a preheated hot broiler until the cheese is bubbling. Serve immediately.

Serves 4
Preparation time: 10 minutes
Cooking time: 15 minutes

GRUYERE AND SHALLOT TOASTS

2 garlic cloves, minced (optional)
2 tablespoons extra-virgin olive oil
1 baguette (French stick), cut diagonally
into 12 x ½-inch thick slices
4 vine-ripened fresh plump tomatoes,
each cut into 3
2 shallots, finely chopped
6 oz Gruyere, Swiss or Cheddar cheese,
shredded, or sliced into ½-oz portions
fine sea salt and freshly ground
black pepper
basil leaves, torn into small pieces,
to garnish

1 Mix the garlic, if using, with the olive oil and brush one side of each baguette slice with it. Toast both sides of the bread under a preheated broiler until highly browned. If necessary, brush a little more oil on the oiled sides of the bread. Top each with a piece of tomato and 1 tablespoon of chopped shallots, season, then top with cheese and season again.

2 Place on an oiled cookie sheet and cook in a preheated oven at 375°F, or under the broiler for 6–8 minutes, until the cheese is bubbling. Sprinkle with basil and serve.

Serves 4
Preparation time: 15 minutes
Cooking time: 6–8 minutes
Oven temperature: 375°F

VARIATION

GOAT'S CHEESE AND MUSHROOM TOASTS

Use mozzarella or goat's cheese. Substitute bell peppers, eggplants, onions or mushrooms for the tomatoes. Top with sun-dried tomatoes or peppers in olive oil.

GRILLED TOMATOES ON CIABATTA

4 firm ripe plum tomatoes
1 teaspoon extra-virgin olive oil
4 thick slices ciabatta, cut diagonally
¼ pound thinly sliced mozzarella
a few shredded basil leaves
salt and pepper

1 Cut the tomatoes in half and brush them with olive oil. Grill over hot coals or place under a preheated broiler until they soften and the skins start to blacken.

2 Toast the ciabatta lightly on both sides, either on a hot grill or under the broiler.

3 Spread the sliced mozzarella over the toasted ciabatta and top with the grilled tomatoes and basil. Season with salt and pepper, and serve immediately.

Serves 4
Preparation time: 5 minutes
Cooking time: 5 minutes

MUSHROOM CROSTINI

This is a good alternative to the more mundane garlic bread. If you can get them, use fresh cepes instead of, or as well as, the fresh mushrooms. They are a delicious topping for crostini.

8 tablespoons extra-virgin olive oil
1 baguette (French stick), cut diagonally into about 16 slices
2 tablespoons chopped fresh cilantro
3 garlic cloves, minced
¼ cup sweet butter
6 oz fresh ceps or open cap mushrooms
4½ tablespoons dry white wine
3 tablespoons freshly shredded Parmesan cheese (optional)
fine sea salt and freshly ground black pepper

1 Use 6 tablespoons of the olive oil for brushing: brush a cookie sheet with the oil and brush both sides of each baguette slice with olive oil. Arrange the slices on the cookie sheet and place under a preheated broiler. Brown both sides carefully—try not to over-cook them, as they burn easily. Remove and cool.

2 Mix the cilantro and garlic. Melt the butter and the remaining 2 tablespoons of olive oil in a skillet. Add the mushrooms and saute for 3 minutes. Add the wine and cook gently to reduce it by half. Lower the heat and stir in the chopped cilantro, garlic and seasoning. Continue to cook gently for about 2 more minutes.

3 Remove from the heat, let cool and chop the mushrooms finely. Stir in the Parmesan, if using, and set aside until ready to use.

4 Crostini are good served cold but even better warmed. Spoon some of the mushroom mixture on to each slice, then heat in a preheated oven at 350°F until the Parmesan has melted. Serve immediately.

Serves: 4
Preparation time: 15 minutes
Cooking time: 15 minutes
Oven temperature: 350°F

BRUSCHETTA

4 thick slices of day-old rustic-style bread
2 garlic cloves, cut
extra-virgin olive oil, to drizzle

1 Toast the bread lightly on both sides, either over a grill or under a hot broiler. Immediately rub the toast all over with the garlic cloves and drizzle with as much olive oil as liked. Serve at once or top with any of the suggested toppings on pages 52–53.

Serves 4
Preparation time: 2 minutes
Cooking time: 3–4 minutes

HOT FOCACCIA SANDWICH

I large loaf focaccia or olive bread
4 artichokes in oil, drained and sliced
I red onion, thinly sliced into rings
¼ pound arugula
½ pound thinly sliced haloumi or
camembert cheese
salt and pepper

Red Hot Mayonnaise:
2 red chiles
2 egg yolks
I tablespoon white wine vinegar
I cup corn oil
2 garlic cloves, minced
¼ cup pine nuts
4 tablespoons shredded Parmesan cheese
8 sun-dried tomato halves in oil

1 To make the red hot mayonnaise, first place the chiles under a preheated hot broiler for 5–7 minutes, turning once, until charred and blistered. Transfer to a plastic bag, close the top tightly and set aside until cool. Rub off the charred skins, slit the chiles open and remove all of the seeds. Set aside. Alternatively, grill the red chiles over hot coals.

2 Whisk the egg yolks and vinegar until slightly thickened. Continue to whisk, adding the corn oil in a thin steady stream until the mixture forms a thick, creamy mayonnaise. Then cover and set aside.

3 Place the garlic, pine nuts and Parmesan in a blender or food processor and puree until smooth. Add the sun-dried tomato halves and the red chiles and puree until smooth. With the motor running, gradually add 3 tablespoons of the reserved oil from the tomatoes. Spoon the blended mixture into a bowl, stir in the creamy mayonnaise, cover and set aside.

4 Slice the focaccia or olive bread in half horizontally. Toast both halves, crumb-side down, on the grill. Spread each half with the red hot mayonnaise. Divide the artichokes between the bread halves and add the red onion, arugula and haloumi or camembert. Sprinkle with salt and pepper to taste and serve at once.

Serves 4
Preparation time: 20 minutes, plus 30–60 minutes marinading time
Cooking time: 6–8 minutes

GRILLED TOMATO AND OLIVE PASTE TOPPING

4 firm ripe plum tomatoes, quartered
extra-virgin olive oil
1 quantity Bruschetta (see page 49)
2 tablespoons olive paste
a few shredded basil leaves
salt and pepper

1 Place the plum tomatoes in a broiler tray with a little olive oil and place under a hot broiler for 10 minutes until they are tender and golden.
2 Prepare the bruschetta.
3 Spread the olive paste over one side of each bruschetta and top with the tomatoes, basil leaves and salt and pepper. Serve at once.

Serves 4
Preparation time: 5 minutes, plus making bruschetta
Cooking time: 14 minutes

EGGPLANT AND CUMIN TOPPING

1 tablespoon cumin seeds
¼ cup extra-virgin olive oil
1 teaspoon grated lemon zest
2 small eggplants
1 quantity Bruschetta (see page 49)
4 oz arugula leaves
1 tablespoon Classic French Dressing
(see page 21)

1 Dry-roast the cumin seeds in a small skillet until they start to pop and give off a smoky aroma. Carefully add the oil and lemon zest, remove from the heat and leave to infuse for several hours. Strain the oil into a bowl and reserve.
2 Trim the eggplants and cut each one lengthwise into 4 thick slices. Brush lightly with the cumin-scented oil and place under a preheated broiler. Cook for 6–8 minutes until charred, turn over and repeat. Let cool to room temperature.
3 Just before serving, prepare the bruschetta. Top with the eggplant slices and drizzle over a little of the cumin oil.
4 Toss the arugula leaves with the French dressing, arrange the leaves over the eggplants and drizzle over the remaining cumin oil. Serve at once.

Serves 4
Preparation time: 5 minutes, plus infusing time and making bruschetta and dressing
Cooking time: 18–30 minutes

ESCAROLE AND GRILLED BELL PEPPER TOPPING

I red bell pepper, cored,
seeded and quartered
I yellow bell pepper, cored,
seeded and quartered
2 tablespoons hazelnut oil
2 garlic cloves, sliced
I tablespoon grated lemon zest
2 tablespoons golden raisins
2 tablespoons flaked hazelnuts
6 oz escarole, shredded
I quantity Bruschetta (see page 49)
salt and pepper

I Broil the pepper quarters for 6–8 minutes on each side until charred and tender. Transfer to a plastic bag and set aside until cool enough to handle. Peel off the skin and slice the flesh. Alternatively, grill over hot coals, turning occasionally.

2 Heat the oil in a skillet, add the garlic, lemon zest, golden raisins and hazelnuts and fry gently for 5 minutes until golden. Add the escarole and cook over a low heat for 5 minutes until tender.

3 Meanwhile, prepare the bruschetta.

4 Divide the escarole mixture between the bruschetta and top with the broiled peppers. Serve at once.

Serves 4
Preparation time: 15 minutes, plus making bruschetta
Cooking time: 18–20 minutes

AVOCADO AND BLUE CHEESE TOASTS

Cut long slanting slices from a whole-wheat French loaf for this simple but unusual appetizer.

4 slices whole wheat bread
I tablespoon butter
I large ripe avocado
I tablespoon lemon juice
freshly ground black pepper
3 oz blue cheese

To Garnish:
8 small lettuce leaves
sprigs of watercress

I Place the bread under a preheated broiler and toast on one side. Lightly butter the untoasted side.

2 Peel and halve the avocado, removing the seed. Cut into quarters, then slice each quarter into 4 pieces.

3 Arrange the slices of avocado on the buttered side of each piece of toast and sprinkle with lemon juice and pepper.

4 Cut the cheese into 4 thin slices and lay one over the avocado slices on each piece of toast.

5 Reduce the broiler to medium and broil the toasts lightly until the cheese is melted.

6 Serve immediately garnished with the lettuce leaves and sprigs of watercress.

Serves 4
Preparation time: 10 minutes
Cooking time: 5 minutes

GRILLED MINI EGGPLANTS WITH HERBED GREEK YOGURT

Little eggplants are usually available in ethnic and gourmet markets. Make the yogurt mixture well ahead, so the flavors blend thoroughly, then serve these mini eggplants with warm pita bread lightly toasted on the grill.

12 mini eggplants
3 tablespoons olive oil
salt and pepper

Herbed Greek Yogurt:
2 tablespoons chopped fresh parsley
2 tablespoons chopped fresh dill weed
2 tablespoons chopped fresh mint
I small red onion, finely chopped
2 garlic cloves, minced
½ cup Kalamata olives, pitted and sliced
2 teaspoons fennel seeds, crushed
I tablespoon capers, chopped
I tablespoon gherkins, finely chopped
finely grated zest and juice of I lime
⅝ cup strained Greek yogurt
salt and pepper

I To make the Herbed Greek Yogurt, mix all the ingredients and set aside.
2 Slice all the mini eggplants in half lengthwise, leaving them attached to their stalks.
3 Using a small brush, coat the eggplants with olive oil. Cook on an oiled barbecue grill over moderately hot coals for about 2–3 minutes on each side.
4 To serve, place the eggplants on a serving dish and spoon over the herbed yogurt.

Serves 4
Preparation time: 20 minutes
Cooking time: 6 minutes

MINI STUFFED MUSHROOMS

50 small open cap mushrooms
¼ pound Brie or creamy cheese, diced
¼ cup butter, softened
¾ cup walnut pieces, finely chopped
2 garlic cloves, minced
2 tablespoons fresh parsley, chopped
a little milk

I Trim the stems off the mushrooms. Chop the stems and put into a bowl with the diced cheese (including the rind), butter, walnuts, garlic, parsley and a little milk. Beat all the ingredients together until well mixed but firm.
2 Place the mushrooms, stem-side up, in a broiler tray lined with kitchen foil. Put a spoonful of the walnut mixture on top of each mushroom, dividing it between them.
3 Place under a preheated broiler for about 5 minutes, until the mushrooms are just tender and the filling is golden and bubbling.

Serves 8–10
Preparation time:10 minutes
Cooking time: 5 minutes

BROILED ONIONS WITH BALSAMIC VINEGAR

6 large red onions
3 tablespoons extra-virgin olive oil
I tablespoon chopped fresh thyme
I tablespoon chopped fresh rosemary
2 garlic cloves, minced
I teaspoon coriander seeds, crushed
4 tablespoons balsamic vinegar
4 tablespoons red wine
I tablespoon clear honey
salt and pepper

I Slice the onions into eighths from the stalk to the root without cutting all the way through, and press open. Place in a broiler tray.
2 Combine the oil, herbs, garlic, coriander seeds and seasoning. Drizzle over the onions and place under a preheated medium-hot broiler for 10–15 minutes, turning the onions occasionally.
3 Mix the vinegar, wine and honey together, pour a little over each onion and broil for a further 5–10 minutes, until the onions are tender. Serve with the glazed juices.

Serves 6
Preparation time: 10 minutes
Cooking time: 15–25 minutes

EGGPLANT DIP

2¼ lb eggplants
4 tablespoons mild olive oil
3 tablespoons lemon juice
2 garlic cloves, minced
¼ cup mild onion, very finely chopped
1½ tablespoons very finely chopped red bell pepper
salt and pepper
warm pita bread or brushetta, to serve (see page 49)

To Garnish:
olive oil
chopped fresh parsley

I Broil the eggplants, turning frequently, until the skin is charred and blistered and the flesh feels soft when the eggplant is pressed. Or grill over hot coals until charred, turning frequently. When cool enough to handle, remove and discard the stalks and skin. Squeeze the flesh gently to expel surplus liquid.
2 Chop the flesh roughly so that it still has some texture. Place in a bowl and pour in the oil. Mix in most of the lemon juice and stir in the garlic, onion, red bell pepper and salt and pepper. Taste and add more lemon juice, if necessary. Cover and chill in the refrigerator for several hours.
3 Return to room temperature a short while before serving so that the puree is not too cold. Spoon it into a flat dish and make a few swirls in the surface with the back of a spoon. Pour a thin trickle of olive oil into the whirls and garnish with chopped parsley. Serve with warm pita bread or use to top bruschetta.

Serves 6
Preparation time: 15 minutes, plus chilling time
Cooking time: 5 minutes

SOUR CREAM DIP WITH POTATO SKINS

⅝ cup sour cream
1 teaspoon snipped fresh chives
4 baked potatoes
olive oil, for brushing
salt and freshly ground black pepper

To Serve:
chopped tomatoes and scallions

1 To make the dip, place the sour cream in a bowl, and stir in the chives. Season to taste. Cover and leave to chill in the refrigerator.
2 Cut each baked potato into quarters lengthwise.
3 Using a teaspoon, scoop out most of the flesh, leaving just a thin layer next to the skin. Brush the skins with oil and place them under a preheated broiler for about 5 minutes, turning occasionally, until crisp and golden.
4 Either sprinkle the skins lightly with salt or provide some salt for guests to help themselves. Serve with the chilled dip, and a bowl of finely chopped tomatoes and scallions, if liked.

Serves 4
Preparation time: 10 minutes, plus chilling time
Cooking time: 5 minutes

RED BELL PEPPER AND GARLIC DIP WITH POTATO SKINS

2 medium red bell peppers, halved and seeded
1 garlic clove
1 tablespoon lemon juice
1 tablespoon olive oil
3 tablespoons fresh white breadcrumbs
4 hot or cold baked potatoes
salt and freshly ground black pepper

1 Place the bell peppers and garlic in a saucepan and add just enough water to cover. Bring to a boil, cover and simmer for 15 minutes or until tender. Drain well and cool.
2 Place in a blender or food processor with the lemon juice and olive oil. Process until smooth.
3 Stir in the breadcrumbs and season to taste.
4 Cut the potatoes into quarters lengthwise. Scoop out most of the flesh. Brush the skins with oil and place under a preheated broiler for about 5 minutes, turning occasionally, until crisp and golden. Serve hot, with the dip.

Serves 4
Preparation time: 10 minutes
Cooking time: 20 minutes

ROUILLE

1 red bell pepper, seeded and chopped
2 garlic cloves, minced
2 red chiles, seeded and chopped
6 tablespoons extra-virgin olive oil
½ cup fresh white breadcrumbs
salt and pepper

1 Put the bell pepper, garlic, chiles and oil in a blender or food processor and process until fairly smooth. Clean down the sides of the bowl to make sure you blend all the ingredients evenly.
2 Add the breadcrumbs, and salt and pepper to taste, and process again to form a thick paste.
3 Transfer to a small bowl, cover and chill until ready to serve.

Makes ½ cup
Preparation time: 10 minutes

MAYONNAISE

2 egg yolks
1 tablespoon white wine vinegar or tarragon vinegar
1 teaspoon Dijon mustard
1¼ cups olive oil
salt and pepper

1 Put the egg yolks in a bowl with the vinegar and mustard. Add ½ teaspoon salt and black pepper. Beat well to a smooth paste.
2 Gradually beat in the oil, adding it a drop at a time at first. When the mixture begins to thicken, pour in the oil in a thin steady stream, beating constantly until all the oil has been added and the mayonnaise is smooth and thick.
3 Alternatively, combine the egg yolks, vinegar, mustard, salt and pepper in a blender or food processor. Process briefly on medium speed, then slowly add the oil through the feeder tube, drop by drop at first, then in a thin steady stream until all the oil has been incorporated and the mayonnaise is smooth and thick.

Makes about 1½ cups
Preparation time: 10–15 minutes

VARIATIONS

GARLIC MAYONNAISE

Add 1–2 cloves minced garlic to the egg yolks.

HERB MAYONNAISE

Add 1 tablespoon chopped mixed herbs. Use herbs such as chives, parsley, tarragon and thyme, and add to the made mayonnaise.

SWEET PEPPER DRESSING

2 red bell peppers
1 garlic clove, minced
1 teaspoon sweet paprika
½ teaspoon mustard powder
4 teaspoons red wine vinegar
½ cup light olive oil
salt and pepper

1 Cook the bell peppers under a preheated broiler for 20 minutes, turning occasionally, until the skins are blistered and blackened all over. Transfer to a bowl, cover with layers of paper towels and set aside. When cool enough to handle, rub off and discard the skins. Cut each bell pepper in half, remove the seeds. Roughly chop.
2 Place the flesh in a blender or food processor. Add the garlic, sweet paprika, mustard and vinegar, with salt and pepper to taste. Process until fairly smooth. With the motor running, slowly pour in the oil until the dressing is smooth. Adjust the seasoning to taste.

Makes 1¼ cups
Preparation time: 5 minutes
Cooking time: 15–20 minutes

WALNUT DRESSING

3 tablespoons balsamic vinegar
or sherry vinegar
1 teaspoon firmly packed brown sugar
1 teaspoon Dijon mustard
½ cup walnut oil
1 tablespoon finely chopped walnuts
1 tablespoon chopped fresh parsley
or other herb, e.g. sage, thyme or basil
salt and pepper

1 Combine the vinegar, sugar and mustard in a small bowl. Add salt and pepper to taste. Stir to mix, then gradually whisk in the walnut oil.
2 Stir the chopped walnuts and herbs into the dressing and adjust the seasoning to taste.

Makes about ⅝ cup
Preparation time: 10 minutes

VINAIGRETTE

1 tablespoon white or red wine vinegar
1 teaspoon Dijon mustard
pinch of sugar
6 tablespoons extra-virgin olive oil
salt and pepper

Put the vinegar, mustard, sugar and salt and pepper into a small bowl and whisk well. Gradually whisk in the oil until the vinaigrette is well blended.

Makes about ⅜ cup
Preparation time: 5 minutes

GARLIC VINAIGRETTE

¾ cup extra-virgin olive oil
¼ cup cider vinegar
2 tablespoons chopped mixed herbs
1 teaspoon clear honey
1 garlic clove, minced
pinch of mustard powder
salt and pepper

Put all the dressing ingredients in a screw-top jar with salt and pepper to taste. Shake well to combine.

Makes 1 cup
Preparation time: 5 minutes

HERB VINAIGRETTE

1 tablespoon white or red wine vinegar
1 teaspoon Dijon mustard
pinch of sugar
2 tablespoons chopped fresh herbs, e.g.
chives, basil, tarragon, chervil, parsley
6 tablespoons extra-virgin olive oil
salt and pepper

Put the vinegar, mustard, sugar, herbs and salt and pepper into a small bowl and whisk well. Gradually whisk in the oil until well blended.

Makes about ¼ cup
Preparation time: 5 minutes

FRESH RASPBERRY VINAIGRETTE

1 cup fresh raspberries
1 teaspoon firmly packed brown sugar
2 tablespoons red wine vinegar
½ teaspoon Dijon mustard
½ garlic clove, minced (optional)
5 tablespoons olive oil
salt and pepper

1 Combine the raspberries, sugar, vinegar, mustard and garlic, if using, in a small bowl. Mash with a fork until the raspberries are pulpy.
2 Using a wooden spoon, press the raspberry mixture through a strainer into a clean bowl. Whisk in the oil and add salt and pepper to taste.

Makes about 1 cup
Preparation time: 10 minutes

WINE MARINADE

⅝ cup red wine
2 tablespoons lemon juice
I onion, sliced thinly
I carrot, sliced thinly
I celery stalk, chopped finely
sprig of parsley
sprig of thyme
I bay leaf
6 black peppercorns, bruised
I garlic clove, minced

I Combine all the ingredients in a large bowl and leave to stand for about 1 hour before adding the food to be marinaded.
2 Use the excess marinade to baste the food during cooking.

Makes about 1¼ cups
Preparation time: 5 minutes, plus 1 hour standing time

ORANGE MARINADE

finely grated zest and juice of I orange
I tablespoon dark soy sauce
3 teaspoons clear honey
½-inch piece ginger root, peeled and minced
salt and pepper

Mix the ingredients together in a jug.

Makes about ¼ cup
Preparation time: 5 minutes
Note: you can make lime or lemon marinade by substituting their finely grated zest and juice instead of orange.

GARLIC AND HERB OIL

2 cups olive oil, preferably virgin olive oil
2 branches rosemary
6 sprigs thyme
I large garlic clove
I green chili
5–6 small red chiles
6 black peppercorns
6 juniper berries

I Pour the oil into a pretty glass bottle, stoppered with a cork for preference.
2 Wash the herbs well and pat them dry. Peel and halve the garlic. Drop the herbs into the bottle, with the garlic, the whole chiles, peppercorns and juniper berries.
3 Seal tightly. Do not use for at least 2 weeks. Do not strain. If making for presents, the cork can be sealed with red sealing wax.

Makes 2 cups
Preparation time: 5 minutes, plus marinading time

INDEX